Yogi Superhero

Time to Rest

Anna Smithers

All rights reserved. No parts of this book may be reproduced in any form by any mechanical means, including photo-copying, recording or information storage and retrieval without written permission from the author. The author, illustrator, and publisher accept no responsibility for any injuries or losses that may result from practicing yoga outlined in the story book. Please ensure your own safety and safety of the children. Yoga is about listening and being kind to your body and mind.

Copyright © 2020 Anna Smithers

All rights reserved.

ISBN: 9798685558640

To all my yoga teachers: past, present and future.

Thank you for everything.

I am a Yogi Superhero,
always ready for adventures high and low,
but sometimes my body gets tired,
and my mind feels like it needs to slow.

To get my energy back,
I need my body and mind to rest,
because only when I am relaxed,
I can be my very best!

I lie down on my back
with my legs out straight,
I wrap a blanket around me,
and feel its comforting weight.

I stretch my arms flat on the floor,
I feel very warm and cosy.
I close my eyes and rest my mind,
even if it's still a bit noisy.

I squeeze all parts of my body
to get the wiggles out,
noticing everything inside me
and watching my body throughout.

Seeing how my mind feels
and noticing all the emotions,
I sense them all at once
and go through different motions.

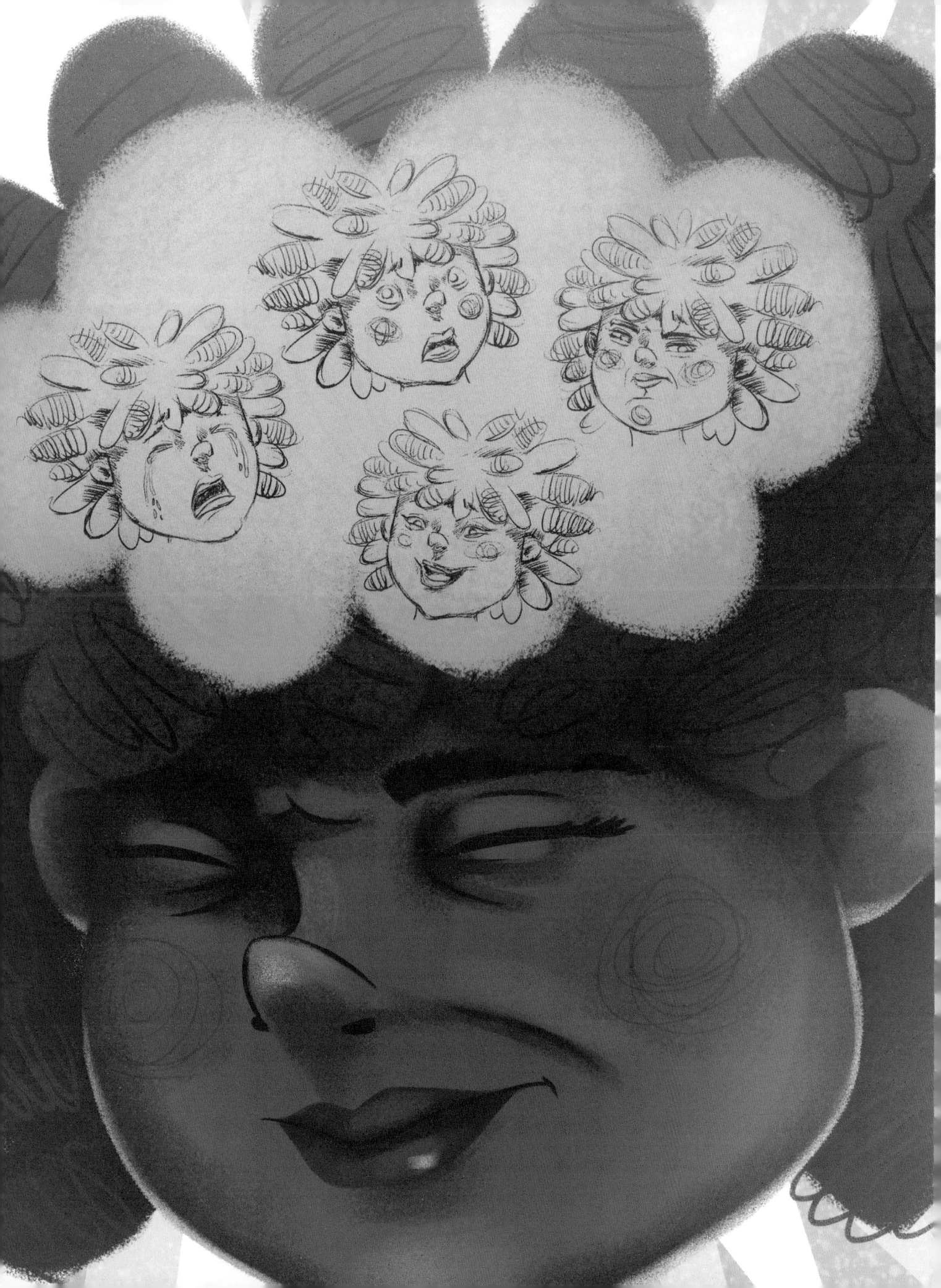

I connect with my breath,
and feel my tummy moving,
breathing deeply through my nose,
my energy is improving.

And with my Yogi Superpowers,
I imagine a bright star in the night sky.
It takes my hand, puts me on a soft cloud,
and I sink in without having to try.

The light of the star is filling up my feet
and my feet become soft.

The light of the star is filling up my legs
and my legs become soft.

The light of the star is filling up my tummy
and my tummy becomes soft.

The light of the star is filling up my chest
and my chest becomes soft.

The light of the star is filling up my back
and my back becomes soft.

The light of the star is filling up my arms
and my arms become soft.

The light of the star is filling up my hands
and my hands become soft.

The light of the star is filling up my neck
and my neck becomes soft.

The light of the star is filling up my head
and my head becomes soft.

The light of the star is filling up my mind
and my mind becomes soft.

Now my body becomes colder,
from my toes to the top of my head,
like stepping in snow with bare feet
- the cold begins to spread.

Slowly my body becomes warmer,
from my toes to the top of my head,
like stretching my feet in front of the fire
- the warmth begins to spread.

I feel my body become lighter,
from my toes to the top of my head,
like I am a light feather floating to the ground
- the lightness begins to spread.

I feel my body become heavier,
from my toes to the top of my head,
like I am made from heavy stone
- the heaviness begins to spread.

With my magic powers,
I feel a spiky ball in my hands,
and the gentle massage of the spikes
throughout my body expands.

With my magic powers,
I feel a soft, silky scarf in my hands,
and the gentle softness of the material
throughout my body expands.

Now I feel my tummy moving,
and on the inbreath expanding,
the sound of my breath calms me down
and it's really quite enchanting.

On my outbreath my tummy gets smaller
and my abdomen is contracting,
my thoughts are slowing right down,
and my emotions stop acting.

My energy is slowly restoring
as my mind and body rests.
I feel my tummy going up and down
for the next 10 breaths.

I start to bring myself back
to the place I am lying,
like on a magic carpet,
it feels like I'm flying.

I start to wiggle my toes
and wiggle my fingers too,
moving my legs from side to side,
sensing my energy renew.

I feel lighter and energised
- for new adventures I am ready.
My body is strong and yet relaxed,
my mind is calm and steady.

I am a Yogi Superhero
who loves adventures and relaxation.
I know with body and mind rested,
I am full of life and inspiration.

Other Yogi Superhero Stories:

Yogi Superhero

Yogi Superhero
Adventures in Nature - Forest

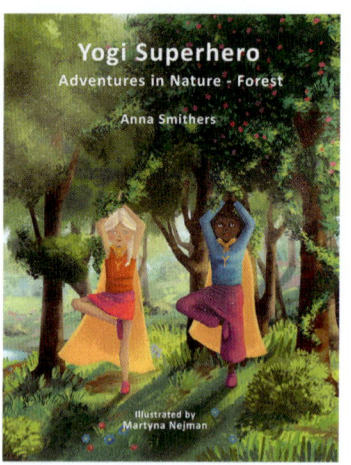

From the Author

Dear Adult - Thank you for reading this book! If you enjoyed it, please consider leaving a review. It would mean the world to me! Thank you.

Hi Children - If you have any ideas for new Yogi Superhero adventures, I would love to hear from you! I also love receiving letters, drawings and pictures. Feel free to email anna@annasmithers.com and I will try my best to email you back!

A. Smithers

Anna Smithers is an author, fully qualified yoga teacher and yoga therapist for children and young adults. She specialises in working with children and people with autism. Anna holds two masters degrees; in Science and Business Management. Her Yogi Superhero Adventures in Nature – Forest won a bronze medal in a children's picture book category in Living Now US Awards 2020.

Martyna Nejman is an illustrator who lives in Warsaw, Poland. She became interested in drawing when she was a teenager, using traditional drawing techniques. Nowadays she mostly uses digital methods. Martyna collaborates with publishers as well as with individual clients. She creates children's illustrations, posters, portraits and book covers. More information on https://martynanejman.wixsite.com/ilustrator-portfolio

Printed in Great Britain
by Amazon